Fear of Frying

RAINCOAST BOOKS

Vancouver

Fear of

James Barber

Frying

with illustrations by the author

Raincoast Books
8680 Cambie Street
Vancouver, B.C.
V6P 6M9
(604) 323-7100

www.raincoast.com

This book was originally published in 1978 by Douglas & McIntyre Ltd.

1 2 3 4 5 6 7 8 9 10

Canadian Cataloguing in Publication Data:

Barber, James, 1923–
Fear of Frying

Includes index.
ISBN 1-55192-310-6

1. Frying. 2. Cookery. I. Title.

TX689.B37 2000   641.7'7   C00-910015-6

Raincoast Books gratefully acknowledges the support of the Government of Canada, through the Book Publishing Industry Development Program, the Canada Council for the Arts and the Department of Canadian Heritage. We also acknowledge the assistance of the Province of British Columbia, through the British Columbia Arts Council.

Printed and bound in Canada.

To Geneviève, with love

Table of Contents

Preface to the New Edition

Way back when, before Martha Stewart, before
e-mail, before gourmet websites, when hair was
long and money was short, it was the summer of
love, a time when everybody wanted to run away
and lots of people didn't because they couldn't
cook. The Beatles had taught us all how simple
music could be, just three chords, so I wrote these
books – quick, simple and easy food that made
cooking almost as much fun as making love and
certainly as easy as strumming a guitar.

The books sold and sold, not just for backpacks but
for boats, cottages and bachelor apartments. They
never turned up at garage sales; people hung on to
them, and I still get regular mail – "Do you still have
a spare copy?" – from people who want to give
them to their kids but won't part with their own.
(An antique book dealer in Victoria recently sold a
mint first edition of *Ginger Tea Makes Friends* for
$350....) So we reprinted. Even today, all you need
to be a good cook is a fry pan and these little books.

James Barber

Introduction

If you're going to buy one thing to cook with, get an electric fry pan – a big one, the biggest you can find. You can bake in it, stew things, steam things, or just plain fry things; make cakes, yogurt, hot-cakes, patés; steam clams, cook crabs, deep-fry your own potato chips, make fantastic hot choco-late, or use it for a fondue pot. And it's portable. You can run away with a fry pan, camp in a motel room for a week, or like a lawyer I know who works late (he really does – this is not a euphemism for an affair), keep one in the desk drawer to cook a little something instead of facing the dreaded basement cafeteria.

Use decent oil. Cold pressed oil (the Italians are more romantic – they call it "virgin") is best, and butter is wonderful, especially mixed with a little oil to keep it from burning. If you use bacon for cooking, save the fat in a can in the fridge (bacon is seventy percent fat anyway).

Always keep a couple of onions under the sink, and a little garlic. Everything else is interchange-able. For any veal recipe you can use pork or chicken. It will taste different but it will taste good. If you don't have wine, use stock or beer. Or water and a bit more seasoning. If you're out of something, send your guests to the corner store; there's nothing in this book that you can't find easily and almost anywhere. Six herbs, six spices, you... and the fry pan.

Danish Scallops

The offering of compassion, like rewards (and punishment) should be immediate. You mustn't make people wait too long when they are in need. And that includes you.

If someone is around to massage your eyebrows (there is nothing more gentling), and maybe to put fresh cut slices of ginger to your temples, they may also be inclined, or persuaded, to let their fingers discover the line of your jawbone beneath your skin, to hold (again very gently, try it on yourself) the bridge of your nose between thumb and forefinger, or just to hold your head quietly between their hands. They won't really cure anything, but it's a lot better than lying on the bed looking at the ceiling and wishing you were dead.

If you want to practice being sad, and learn how it feels to have all those gentle massages taking place inside instead of outside, then this way of doing scallops is a good beginning. A discreet and gentle use of curry; the spiciness is there as a pleasant reminder of things to come.

African Chicken

I was trying to copy a dish dimly remembered from a Malaysian restaurant. And she was a newspaper lady with a smile, a hat and white gloves, a real ladies' pages newspaper lady looking for scoops on engagements, deviant dress patterns in non-June brides, and household hints for the have-nots.

She was delighted, thrilled, and thought everything was "darling." It was the first time, she said, that she had ever been in a real artist's studio. She took off her gloves, her hat and her coat. And sat on the cat.

I offered Band-Aids, but she wouldn't let me look. The interview was somewhat shorter than I expected, and so was the piece in the paper. She called my dish African Chicken. I suppose it's hard to get things correct when you're standing up to type.

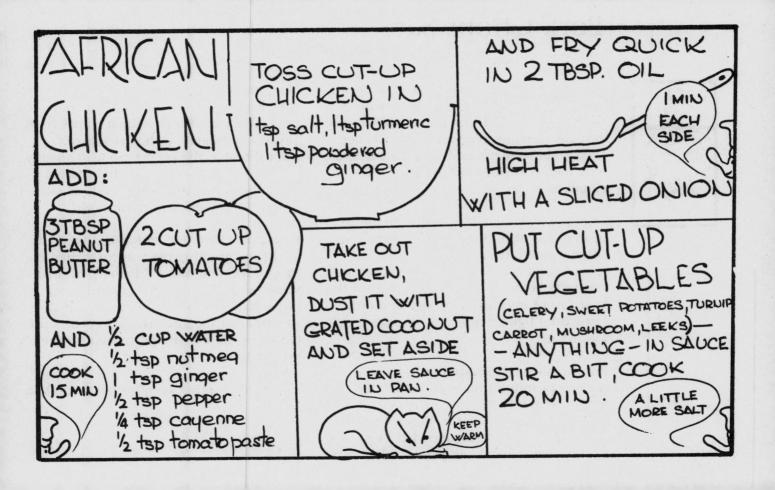

Pork Chops Sate

My mother, who is seventy-five, has just discovered the joys of illicit love, which she chooses to call "my friend." She blushes like a teenager every time he calls her "Dear," and she pretends in public not to look happy in case my father parts the clouds and sees her.

The joys that come late in life are not to be despised. It took me fifteen years to discover women, twenty to get hooked on tobacco and another fifteen to get off it. I was forty before mushrooms expanded the horizons of my consciousness, and only last week I figured out how to make it on a waterbed.

But the most significant discovery of my life was peanut butter, courtesy of the United States Air Force, which seemed never to travel without it. When I tasted my first peanut butter sandwich I was twenty-two years old and since then have become an addict.

Not peanut butter and jelly, certainly not with bananas, just plain old crunch – preferably Deaf Smith (which comes from Texas) – untreated, unhomogenized peanut butter, the good kind which really sticks to your teeth, on toasted whole wheat bread, with just a sprinkle of salt on it; the finest breakfast in the world.

If you were Javanese you would spend a long time grinding peanuts for dishes like this, unless you had a Cuisinart, roasted your own fresh nuts and ground them immediately into peanut butter. But all supermarket shelves have jars of the stuff. Once you start to use peanut butter there's no end to it.

And as my mother says, it's never too late to start.

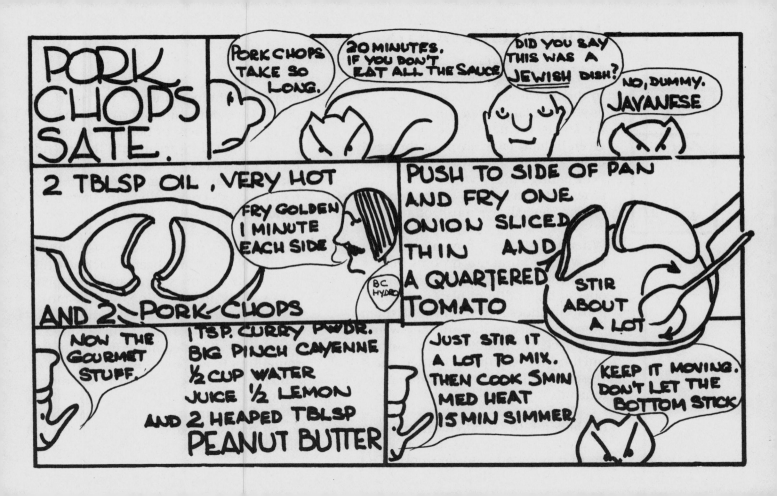

Mmmushrooms

4

In the mornings early, before the paper-boy, in the fall and in the spring, and on the lawns, the newly made wonderful green billiard table lawns of the newly mortgaged, in subdivisions called Whispering Pines – where perhaps two pines did once, before the bulldozers, exist – there were always mushrooms.

When I was a small boy my uncle showed me where to find mushrooms in cow pastures, and we brought them home, big ones as big as dinner plates and thick as platform shoes. We would cook them slowly, in bacon fat, until they were dark and black, the middles oozing juice and a smell from them that if bottled and called "Essence de Breakfast" would make a parfumeur's fortune.

If you comb the subdivisions (which have all used topsoil brought in from cow pastures) you are quite likely to find a good crop of field mushrooms at the right time of the year, but you must go early before the crows eat them or before the house-proud owners kick them into the lavender bushes. They taste pretty good, when you can find them. But remember the mushroom picker's creed: When in doubt, chuck it out.

In the supermarkets there are now mushrooms that have not been bleached white – big brownish ones three and four inches across. They are good, too. But the most lily white and virginal mushrooms can also be made into a flavourful textured, thoroughly dignified meal, instead of just something to add to a steak, if you remember to cook them with the lid on. That was my uncle's secret. Sprinkle them with a little lemon juice if you want to be super-sophisticated, or use basil instead of tarragon. Just be kind and just be gentle.

Hurry Curry

5

There are nights when you don't win the lottery, right?

And somebody has a six-pack in the trunk, which does very well to tide you over, while somebody else goes to find another dozen. During which time you cook dinner.

Sprinkling grated coconut over this curry is not going to please the purists, but then if you're into six-packs and lottery tickets you aren't going to be hanging out with too many purists, right? Frying the curry powder before you add anything else is important; it blends the spices and smoothes them out. The best Indian cooks cook their spices for hours, very, very slowly, and keep them as carefully as you look after your personal stash. They call it masala, and there are as many versions of masala as there are recipes for the perfect martini.

If you don't like, can't stand or haven't got beer, lhassi (see recipe) is a truly remarkable complement to curry.

Consider the Oyster
(an homage to M.F.K. Fisher)

The less done to oysters the better. I like to sit at low tide in a big pool by a big rock at a beach on Hornby Island. With an oyster knife, a friend and a bottle of champagne. A bottle of Guiness' Stout will also do, or a good dark healthy vitamin-packed beer of any kind. We have, before the champagne ran out, remembered forty apiece, straight out of the sea, out of the shell and into paradise.

Very few restaurants are to be trusted with an oyster. They don't have time to be gentle, to carefully watch, to feel for them, to understand them. There is one marvelous oyster dish, Huîtres Prince Albert, in a Vancouver restaurant called Le Napoleon, and they manage to retain the texture and the taste of the sea, but that kind of treatment is rare.

And now you can do it. When we did this on television I received over 2,000 letters. The nicest one said "Sir, you are wicked. I love you." See what trouble a little simplicity can get you into.

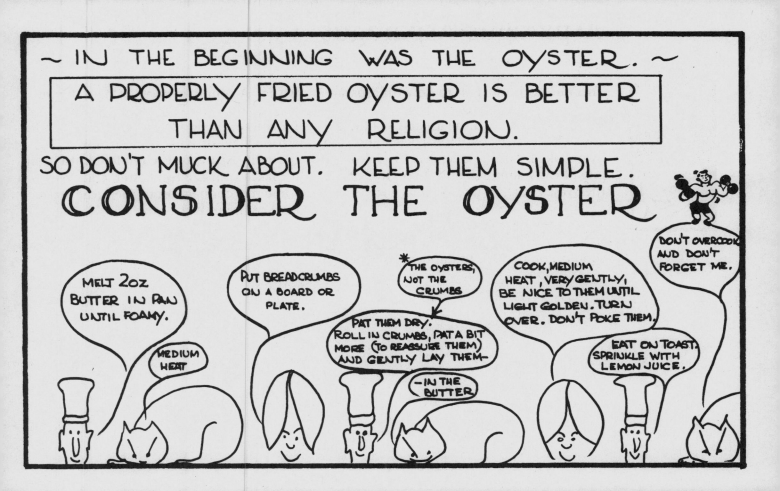

Asparagus-Asparagus

7

This has nothing at all to do with asparagus in cans or with frozen asparagus, and even less to do with the asparagus of the gourmet kitchens which is peeled and overcooked. This asparagus is the fresh one of early summer, and if you live on the West Coast, of late summer too.

This is the asparagus of total luxury, an overindulgence you can afford then and should not attempt to duplicate in mid-winter. A couple of slices of ham, if you have to eat meat with it, or a lovely Piccata di Vitello (page 41) if you want to astonish guests with your virtuosity. But basically asparagus is complete unto itself; it makes your life feel better, and gives you some real connection to the great master plan of the universe.

Even the morning after, asparagus reminds you of what a good time you had.

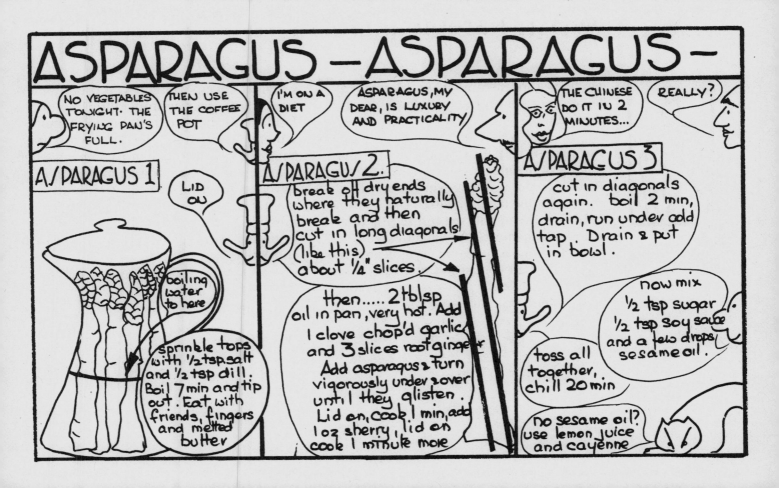

Welsh Rarebit

No bookstore is complete without its collection of stuff on the interpretation of dreams.

But there is very little written on the provoking of dreams. Which is where Welsh Rarebit comes into its own. For a full colour double feature, with a cast of thousands, with you yourself in the title role, with your favourite desiderata playing opposite you, and a good complicated plot dragging in all your secret neuroses, there is nothing to beat a really late night supper of Welsh Rarebit.

Cheddar cheese will give you good domestic stuff, all the way from Doris Day to Jane Fonda. Imported cheese will require either a facility in foreign languages, or subtitles, or the blind faith you have when watching Chinese Kung-Fu movies. I've never tried a little curry powder in it, mainly because I can't stand those interminable Indian flicks featuring the Collected Works of William Shakespeare in Hindi.

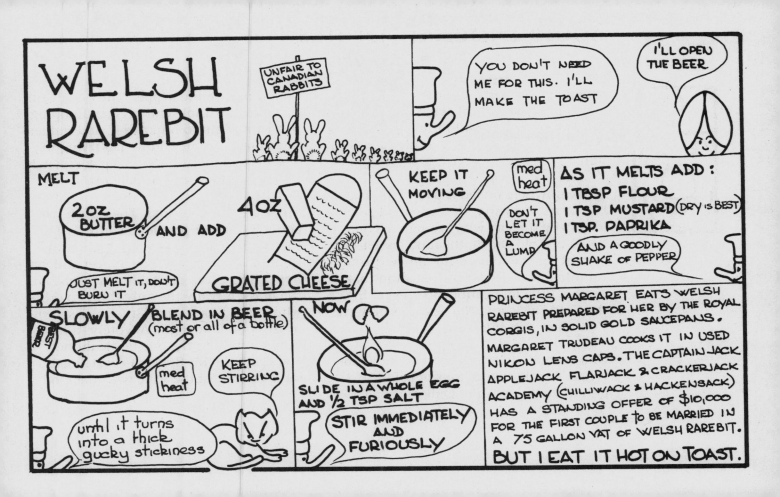

Some Different Drinks

When I give a party, no matter what my guests bring they drink what I give them, and their bottles go into the cupboard under the sink to be used at my discretion.

Booze unwisely mixed is bad news. The last hours of a party, the Scotch all gone (drunk by the guy who brought a $1.35 bottle of Cold Duck), the food gone too (except for the sour cream dip) and you get into a half-decent conversation that needs a little lubrication. So you get into the Cold Duck, and the next morning the Cold Duck gets into you.

Or somebody tells your host about a marvelous punch: two gallons of cold tea, a pint of vodka, a can of Quik and half a pound of cayenne pepper. The first guests find it undrinkable and suggest dumping in a case of gin to improve it, and suddenly you're all in the county jail trying to walk a straight line after being completely unable to blow into the balloon.

These are honest drinks. The punch has enough taste for people to control what they're doing, the shandy is a first class solution to drinking enough beer and yet not falling asleep on a summer afternoon, the lhassi is really the only thing to drink with curried food, and Kir (all purists will insist upon Bourgogne Aligoté) is a first class solution to the one-bottle dinner. You drink the Kir first as a cocktail and serve the rest of the wine with the food.

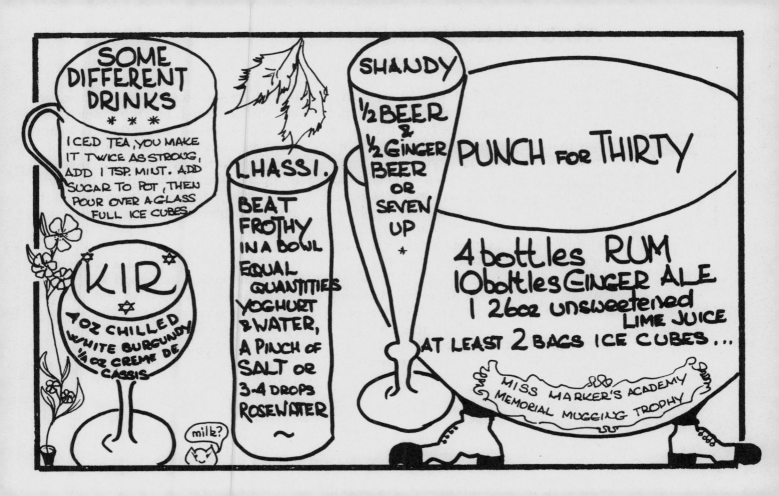

Arab Pitta Bread

Everybody has a friend somewhere with an oven, right? This is the only non-top-of-the-stove recipe in the book, the minor flaw that the Japanese build into each of their works of art. And if you haven't got a friend with an oven, then you baby-sit one; put an advertisement in the laundromat, or even just watch the faces in your apartment building – the harried ones with the chewed bottom lips are the ones in need of your services.

And while they are at the movie, you and their kids make bread. Most of the time you can watch TV, because there is really very little effort to bread making, and there is an enormous calm that comes from it.

Just before the bread goes into the oven, if you decide there is much too much, separate each little flat loaf with waxed paper, stack the loaves and put them into the freezer. Next time you want fresh and immediate bread, take out a couple, let them sit to defrost while you heat up the oven and the cookie sheets, then whang them in.

A big stew and pitta bread, a barbecue with pitta bread, Greek food with pitta bread, even just a big salad and pitta bread. Very, very easy.

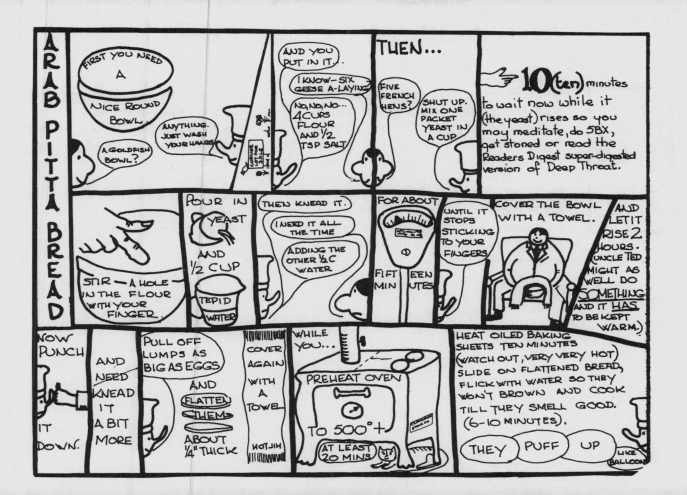

Party Stuff

Something has to happen at a party. Something more than a can of peanuts and a bottle of Scotch. We have parties in the steam baths, parties at midnight in the children's playground, wonderful parties on the 3:00 a.m. ferry from Vancouver to Nanaimo. (There's never anybody on it, but it has to go back for a full load of commuters next morning, and there's a rocking horse in the front lounge still wired for nickels).

We have parties on the beach, up the mountain, and on the fire escape. Everybody else brings booze. I bring food. And get invited to a lot of parties.

The peanut butter number needs to be made in large quantities. It keeps, but it seldom gets a chance to. You'll never touch an onion soup mix dip again.

PARTY STUFF

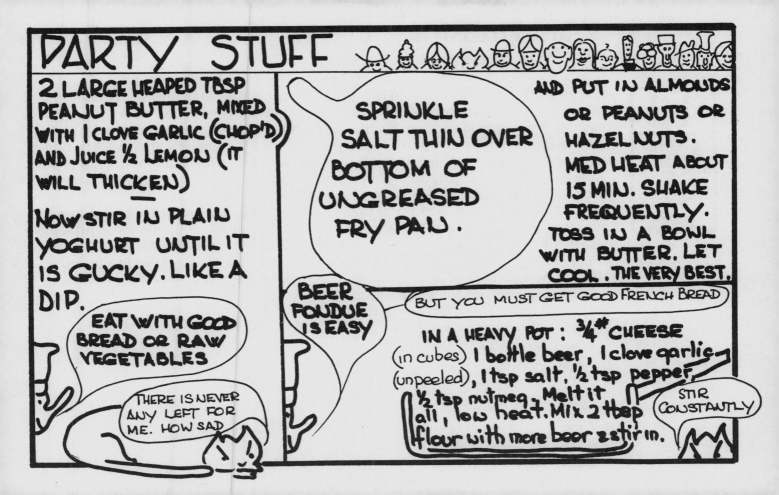

2 LARGE HEAPED TBSP PEANUT BUTTER, MIXED WITH 1 CLOVE GARLIC (CHOP'D) AND JUICE ½ LEMON (IT WILL THICKEN)

NOW STIR IN PLAIN YOGHURT UNTIL IT IS GUCKY. LIKE A DIP.

EAT WITH GOOD BREAD OR RAW VEGETABLES

THERE IS NEVER ANY LEFT FOR ME. HOW SAD

SPRINKLE SALT THIN OVER BOTTOM OF UNGREASED FRY PAN.

AND PUT IN ALMONDS OR PEANUTS OR HAZEL NUTS. MED HEAT ABOUT 15 MIN. SHAKE FREQUENTLY. TOSS IN A BOWL WITH BUTTER. LET COOL. THE VERY BEST.

BEER FONDUE IS EASY

BUT YOU MUST GET GOOD FRENCH BREAD

IN A HEAVY POT: ¾# CHEESE (in cubes) 1 bottle beer, 1 clove garlic (unpeeled), 1 tsp salt, ½ tsp pepper, ½ tsp nutmeg. Melt it all, low heat. Mix 2 tbsp flour with more beer & stir in.

STIR CONSTANTLY

Salad Dressings

It's not all that complicated; you don't need a $200 Cuisinart, or a twenty-speed blender, not even a fancy French whip. All you need to free yourself forever from the bondage of the bottled salad dressings (you know how they hang around in the fridge, an inch of blue cheese and a bit less of Italian and some weird stuff that the label fell off of and you don't know whether it's suntan lotion gone sour or the cream that Doctor Whatsit gave you the time you both went to see him but it was a false alarm), all you need is a spice jar, one of those nice little ones that the Spice Islands oregano comes in.

Put the stuff in, screw the lid on – unless you want your friends to lick the dressing off you and shake it well. That's all. (You can use the same technique for blending flour or cornstarch and water to thicken a sauce.)

Just shake it well, stick your finger in to taste it, and fix it up the way your tongue tells you to, remembering never to put it on green salads until just before you're going to eat. That way the greens stay fresh.

Some Salads

Edith Sitwell was a snotty, uppity, frightfully rich and even more pretentious lady of the avant-garde art scene in Britain who (along with Dylan Thomas and sundry other literary drunks) was among the first of the electronic age shock troops to visit North America and lecture to the culture hungry.

When she went back to England her friends said, "Tell us, dahling, do tell us about America." "My deahs," she replied, "it was one cocktail party after another."

"And what"(the Brits are rather like this) they asked, "is a cocktail party?"

"Peanuts," she answered. "Peanuts, whiskey and an infinity of boredom."

But they pressed her even more for some facts concerning life on this side of the Atlantic. Any fact, in fact.

"Well, my deahs," (and nobody every worked out whether it was her eyebrows which pulled her nose up or the nose which pushed from beneath) "it appeared to me that any given moment fifty percent of the population was eating the same dreary lettuce."

It doesn't have to be, it doesn't have to be, despite what your Home Ec teacher told you.

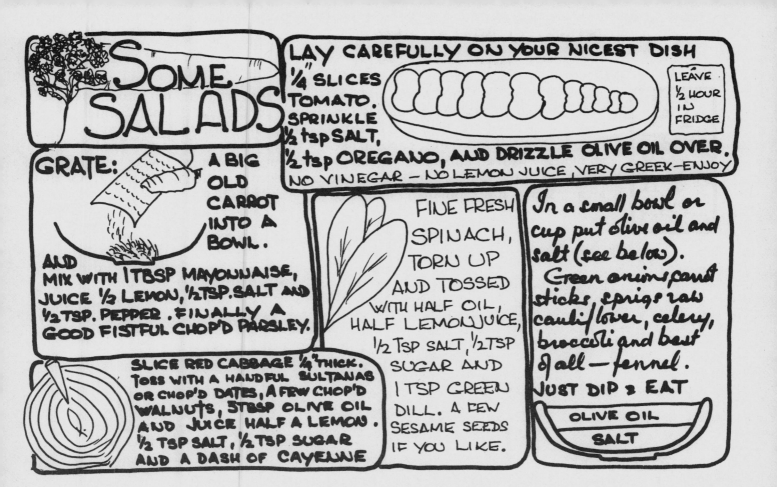

SOME SALADS

LAY CAREFULLY ON YOUR NICEST DISH ¼" SLICES TOMATO. SPRINKLE ½ tsp SALT, ½ tsp OREGANO, AND DRIZZLE OLIVE OIL OVER.
NO VINEGAR — NO LEMON JUICE, VERY GREEK — ENJOY

LEAVE ½ HOUR IN FRIDGE

GRATE: A BIG OLD CARROT INTO A BOWL.

AND MIX WITH 1 TBSP MAYONNAISE, JUICE ½ LEMON, ½ TSP. SALT AND ½ TSP. PEPPER. FINALLY A GOOD FISTFUL CHOP'D PARSLEY.

SLICE RED CABBAGE ¼" THICK. TOSS WITH A HANDFUL SULTANAS OR CHOP'D DATES, A FEW CHOP'D WALNUTS, 3 TBSP OLIVE OIL AND JUICE HALF A LEMON. ½ TSP SALT, ½ TSP SUGAR AND A DASH OF CAYENNE

FINE FRESH SPINACH, TORN UP AND TOSSED WITH HALF OIL, HALF LEMON JUICE, ½ TSP SALT, ½ TSP SUGAR AND 1 TSP GREEN DILL. A FEW SESAME SEEDS IF YOU LIKE.

In a small bowl or cup put olive oil and salt (see below). Green onions, carrot sticks, sprigs raw cauliflower, celery, broccoli and best of all — fennel. JUST DIP & EAT

OLIVE OIL
SALT

Risotto Milanese

The simplest of all dishes. A care-and-nurturing recipe. A kind dinner. There is a hypnotic quality to the slow and careful turning. None of this frantic dabbing like an old lady with an umbrella trying to get a cow out of the garden, but a considerate, loving, Strauss waltz round and rounding. The more care you put into it, the more velvety the result. It is indeed remarkable, the sort of dish that is so simple to learn and so disproportionately productive of a reputation. You will never again be forced back to that tired old lasagna recipe that everybody has.

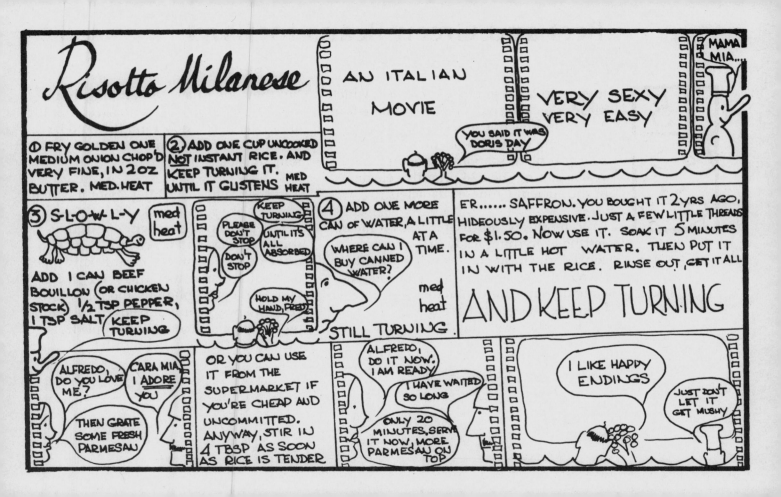

Beef and Green Beans for Two

If you can learn to do this properly, which means quickly, you will have mastered the first technique of Chinese cooking, without having to buy a wok, or taking a course at night school, or spending five years learning the 224 primitive elements of the ancient Chinese characters.

Basically this is "stir-frying," and it means getting everything ready first, the rice cooked, the meat cut, everything right there, and the people with their tongues hanging out. Chinese food is nothing you keep hot; the guests have to wait for it, not the other way round.

But they don't have to wait long. I can have dinner on the table fourteen minutes after I get in the door, and it would be sooner if the rice didn't take exactly that long to cook.

And the really great thing about it is that you feel like such a cook. It's magic – dinner seems to come straight out of the shopping bag. And it's cheap – how else can a quarter pound of meat feed two people? But do remember, this is a dish for two. Don't get ambitious and make it for your in-laws, your best beloved's sister, her roommate and a couple of people from the office. That way lies disaster.

BEEF and GREEN BEANS FOR TWO

PREPARE THREE THINGS:

1. MEAT
SLICE ¼ lb flank steak very thin across grain and toss with 1 tsp corn starch, 1 tsp oil and 1 oz sherry

2. BEANS
BREAK 1 lb fresh green beans into 2" lengths, AND CUT 1 bunch green onions, 1" long

3. CHOP:
1 clove garlic and cut 3 slices fresh ginger.

FRY PAN or WOK VERY HOT.

POUR IN 2 TBSP OIL

AND TOSS MEAT ABOUT 30 SECONDS

JUST UNTIL IT CHANGES COLOR

AND TIP

INTO HOT BOWL

KEEP MOVING, THE QUICKER YOU DO THIS THE BETTER IT TASTES

NOW QUICK, PAN VERY HOT, 3 TBSP OIL, FRY GINGER & GARLIC 20-30 SECONDS, ADD BEANS, FRY 3 MIN.

KEEP IT ALL TURNING AND VERY HOT

ADD BEEF, ½ TSP salt, ½ tsp pepper

TOSS IT ALL, VERY HOT, OVER & OVER, 1 MINUTE

EAT WITH RICE

McDonald's Hamburger

One day all the meat in North America will be trucked to Chicago and poked down a big hole, under which is a thirty-six zillion horsepower blender.

The meat will all be ground to the same squished bland tastelessness as cat food and then pumped, in stainless steel pipes, to every street corner in the world, where, if you put a dollar in a slot, a bun will drop down and splat – there's your hamburger.

To stave off that evil day...

Shio Yaki

Shio Yaki. (I spelled it wrong in the drawing but the drawing looked so nice!)

Salt has a bad reputation.

Lot's wife got turned into a pillar of it, which in those days, salt being so rare, must have made a wealthy man of Lot, a fact that Genesis omits to mention.

Shio Yaki is essentially Japanese cooking. It is a good summer dish for the long hot sweaty days, and salt on its own (no other seasonings) is a flavour all too seldom appreciated. Don't shove it about in the pan – let it form a glaze.

Clams Daniel

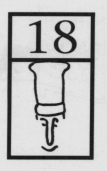

Daniel was a waiter. And Daniel liked to eat. He liked to eat a little more and a little better than most people. So he learned to cook. Which made him an even better waiter because when people asked him "What is...?" he would tell them. They would be impressed because he had a French accent, surprised to get an answer, and generally grateful because waiters sometimes tend to put their noses on high beam and make you feel stupid.

Their gratitude made Daniel a lot of money: He decided to become a restaurateur, to open his own joint, to become the employer of waiters. And then make much more money, in much less time.

But Daniel found that it would have been easier to walk across Lake Ontario than to make money in a restaurant, and that operating a twenty-four-hour day care centre would have given him more time.

Daniel now runs a fishing boat. He makes this dish for himself. He used to make it for his customers. Nobody knew it came out of a can.

And if you don't tell them either....

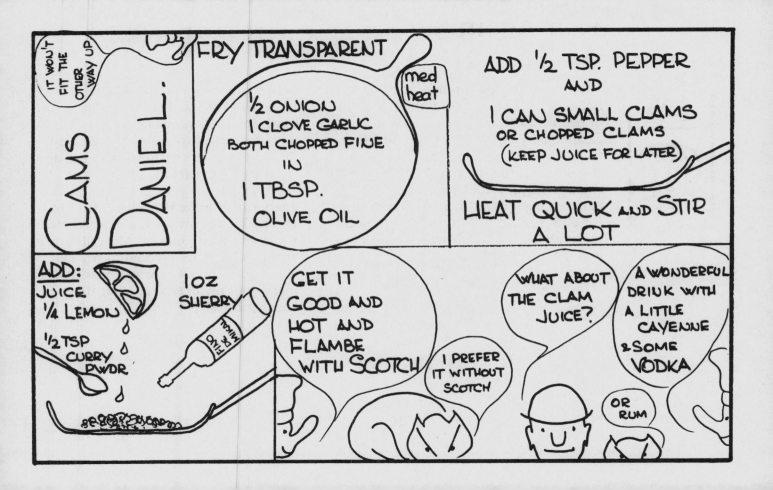

Fish Again

There is an art to the proper mashing of potatoes. A big dollop of butter, and lots of pepper. Nothing else, no milk, no cream, just you, the potatoes and a fork.

It's tough on the wrist, unless you are a championship grade arm-wrestler or maybe a bass player in a rock group, but the end product is fluffy and light, nothing at all like instant potatoes or machine-mashed ones.

When you cook potatoes, or rice, always make twice as much as you'll need. And mash the potatoes while they're hot. Next day you make fish cakes, or Shepherd's Pie, or you mix 'em up with an egg and fry them for breakfast.

Every time I make fish cakes I turn to the East and make my apologies (forehead to the floor, three times) to Mister Heinz for all the bad things I've said in my life about ketchup. Of course, if you want to make your own ketchup – but that's another book.

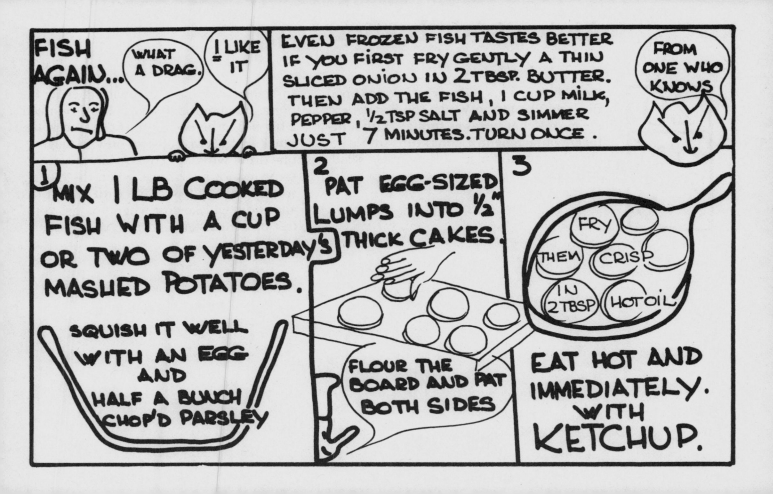

Matelote de Fevrier

Good bread, a good dry white wine (I particularly like Vinho Verde, the Portuguese green one that tastes as though with a little encouragement it could turn into champagne) and a good leafy green salad.

In France they make this with cognac; I prefer rye. Bourbon is good too. You need a big pot, it helps if your friends help, it's quick and it's easy so you only manage one drink while it's cooking and there's some left for afterwards, when the talking starts. Whiskey first, wine with the dinner, and more whiskey for when you get your feet up on the table.

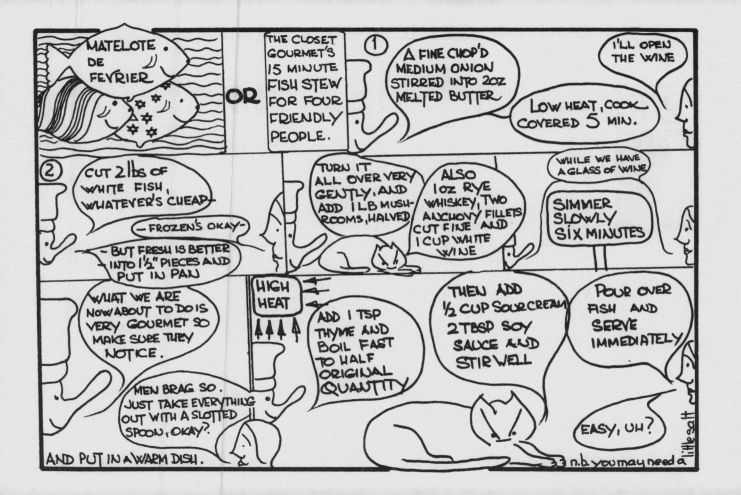

Sort of Soufflé

This is not the greatest soufflé in the world, elegantly presented in a porcelain soufflé dish, its creator stuffed with Valium but still chewing her fingernails down to the first knuckle.

It was invented one marvelous October night, a full moon and a thirty-five-knot wind from the East, the decks awash and the dinghy blown away, Geneviève at the wheel, the C.B.C. pounding out "Der Fliengende Holländer" for us, the boat with the rail under and the crew tied on.

You don't have to have your apartment floor tilted at a forty-five degree angle, you don't have to wear gloves to eat it (even Toronto in mid-winter is not as cold as a sailboat at midnight) and you don't have to be as desperate as I was to prove to somebody that anything is possible, even a sort of soufflé .

But do beat the whites good and stiff, and do fold them in carefully. Your audience will be just as grateful as our crew was.

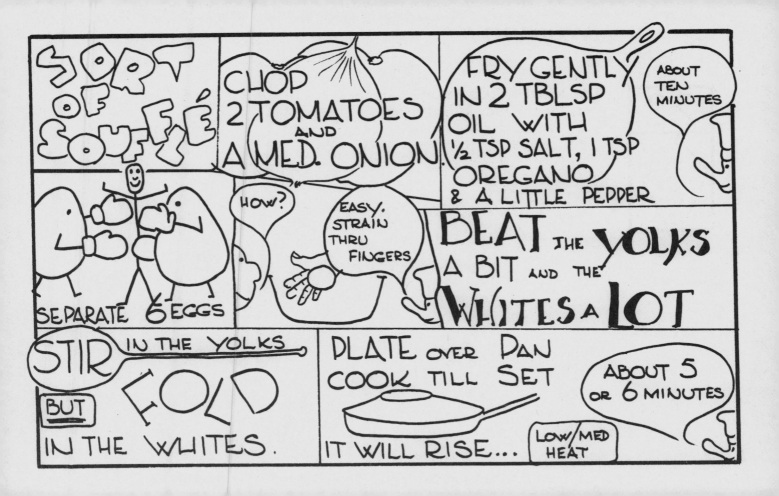

Avocado

This dessert is God's way of saying She's sorry for inventing instant coffee.

Two Quickies for Dessert

23

You don't have to invite people in for dinner. Let them get it elsewhere. Ask them to come around nine (which is when the real talk starts anyway) for dessert.

They arrive full of their own booze, with food they chose themselves; they're happy (and so are you because you spent two hours in the bath, both of you listening first to a little Brahms, perhaps the Clarinet Quintet, and then the Dvořák Cello Concerto, the Fournier one), and they are anticipatory, because everybody waits for dessert.

Which is the ideal climate for entertaining. You should of course be careful, if you live alone, not to fall into the habit of making chocolate fondue just for yourself, because that way lies chocoholism, the dread disease of once slender blondes who have to run miles every day to keep the symptoms from showing.

Even after a movie – four of you – it's easy enough to pick up some chocolate chips in the all-night store. Everybody loves dessert. As the Anglos say in Quebec, *chacun à son "goo."*

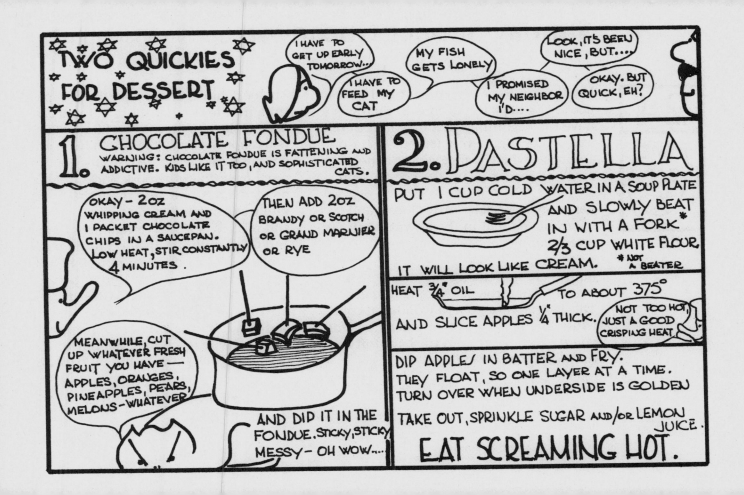

Sunday Supper Cheap

24

If you want to be extravagant and find a goose or a duck to put in this, then you have the beginnings of a magnificent dish called cassoulet, a very famous dish from Toulouse, where France's most famous cooks all seem to have their restaurants.

Beans are a specialty of Toulouse, and it seems fitting that in the town there is also a very famous music school.

But we are not talking about cassoulet, which takes forty-eight hours to prepare. This is very close to it, a wonderful cold winter night supper to let you all pretend you have come in from the back forty to thaw out your noses.

The pork hocks are usually the cheapest thing in the butcher shop, but you can add smoked sausage if you like, or (most marvellous) smoked pork loin, which the delicatessens call Kassler. And if you want more meat than the pork hocks offer, a picnic ham is fine. It's one of those infinitely expandable, non-stopwatch, nice and relaxed, stir it occasionally, sit around and talk, eat it off Salvation Army plates suppers that needs a loaf of really good bread to go with it, any kind of booze at all, and some fresh fruit for dessert.

Best of all, it's the kind of supper that makes people react quite happily to the suggestion that they wash their own dishes.

SATURDAY	**SUNDAY** (SUPPOSING SUPPER AT 6).
BEG, BUY OR BORROW	
BUTTER	**3PM** HOCKS IN COLD WATER, WELL COVERED. SIMMER
5 SMOKED PORK HOCKS	
CELERY	
ONIONS & GARLIC	**4PM** ADD BEANS. SIMMER
PARSLEY	
LEEKS (OPTIONAL)	**5PM** ADD 5 CARROTS
2 LB CAN TOMATOES	(½" PIECES) 3 ONIONS (SLICED)
TOMATO PASTE (SMALL)	4 CLOVES GARLIC (WHOLE)
3-4 LB CABBAGE	6 STALKS CELERY (½")
CARROTS	PARSLEY (A STRING ROUND IT)
FLOUR	THIN SLICED LEEKS. SIMMER.
THYME	
AND SOAK 3 CUPS	**5.30** ADD TOMATOES AND
WHITE BEANS IN	TOMATO PASTE, SIMMER.
6 CUPS COLD WATER	

6.00 ADD CABBAGE, ¼" SLICES. SIMMER.

6.15 MELT 2 OZ BUTTER, ADD 3 TBLSP. FLOUR. MED. HEAT, STIR A LOT UNTIL IT IS LIGHT COFFEE COLOR. ADD A CUP OF BROTH FROM POT, SLOWLY, STIRRING WELL, THEN ANOTHER, THEN POUR EVERYTHING INTO POT WITH BEANS & STUFF. STIR A BIT, SIMMER 15 MIN.

6.30 SKIN HOCKS (HOT, WATCH YOUR FINGERS), ADD A LOT OF PEPPER, SALT (TASTE FIRST) AND 1 TSP THYME.

(BETTER THEY WAIT THAN SUPPER WAITS)

6.45 SERVE 12

LETS GET A LOT OF PEOPLE IN FOR SUNDAY SUPPER - CHEAP.

SIAMESE NAVY

Lazy Man's Chicken

25

Everybody knows about Archimedes jumping out of his bath and rushing naked up the main street of Syracuse when he first figured out the law of flotation.

But history books are strangely silent upon his second discovery, which was how to cook a chicken with hardly any work and almost no energy.

Which I now, in the humility becoming a classical scholar, present to you, proving that the Canada Council (having contributed nothing to this book) might not have wasted its (and your) money had it chosen to subsidize me. I also take the opportunity to thank my mother, who is still wondering whether or not all that education was worthwhile, and consistently urges me to take up a respectable profession, preferably one that requires the wearing of a suit to an office, and certainly one that offers a regular paycheque.

You can't go wrong with this. You don't even have to use a whole chicken; it works with chicken breasts (of course they have no hole to put the spoons in) or whatever assorted pieces you care to collect from the butcher. The timing is for a whole chicken; however, if it's pieces you are using, add just a little more water. You can throw an onion in too, cut up a bit, and a carrot. Keep the broth; it makes a good soup base for the next day. Or you can hot it up for a preface to the chicken dinner, salt it a little, throw in a handful of finely chopped fresh vegetables, almost anything such as a tomato or some leeks, some pasta if you have it – but what comes out will be chicken soup. Presto, you're a Jewish mother.

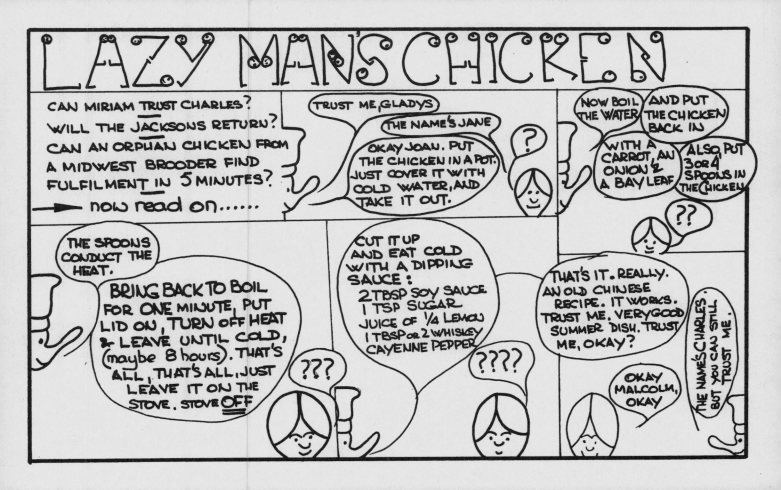

Immanuel Kant's Famous 2 Pork Chops, Some Celery and 2 Big Old Carrots Recipe

26

Pimps, dope dealers, writers, drunks and neurotics head most parents' lists of people their kids should not get mixed up with, along with actors, gays, Marxists, bikers, environmentalists and chicken egg sexers.

But nobody worries about philosophers. And the universities are turning them out almost as fast as McDonald's is making hamburgers – nice, healthy, ordinary-looking people, who can be discovered washing dishes, digging ditches, selling sofas in department stores, baby-sitting, dog-walking, washing cars, sweeping the floors of newspaper offices and (the luckiest and least offensive of them) sitting soulfully behind the counter of small bookstores, reading themselves into functional blindness. They like to eat, although they are not concerned with the process any more than a car cares about which gas pump.

They also like to talk. And talk and talk and talk. If you should find yourself involved with philosophers, the trick is to find them something simple to do while they are talking. Sit them in a chair, or prop them up against the kitchen counter, give them simple and unequivocal instructions (otherwise they are likely to get involved in the semantics of seasonings) and keep them moving.

If they insist that you become involved in their conversations, long words are not necessary. "Possibly," or "But on the other hand," with a little doubt thrown in for luck, or even the carefully timed raising of eyebrows, all are sufficient to set them off for another fifteen minutes.

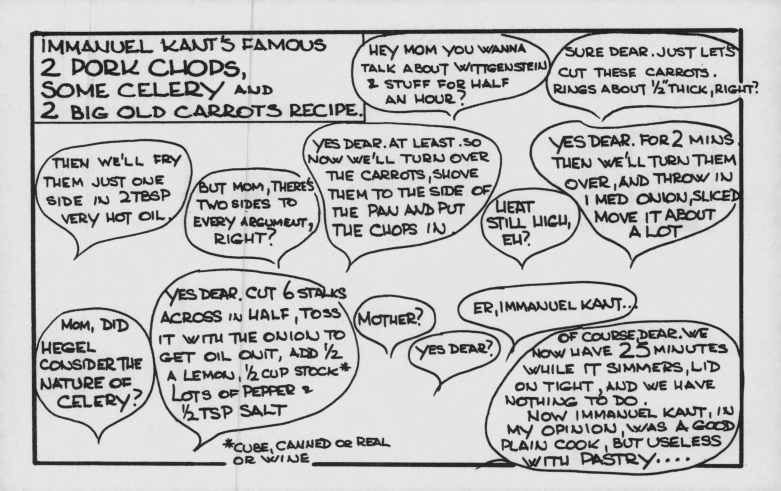

Super Sausages

Round the back of Victoria Station the hot chestnut men park their barrows at night. And the sandwich board men, those unfortunates who walk up and down with boards back and front advertising the least savoury of restaurants. (At least they used to. Nowadays they tout the virtues of massage parlors and pornographic picture parlors.)

When I was young and given to drink, a habit which frequently resulted in missing the last train home, I frequently slept among the hot chestnut men. And ate 3:00 a.m. suppers with them. "Bangers," the British call sausages. Mostly they eat them with mashed potatoes. This is better.

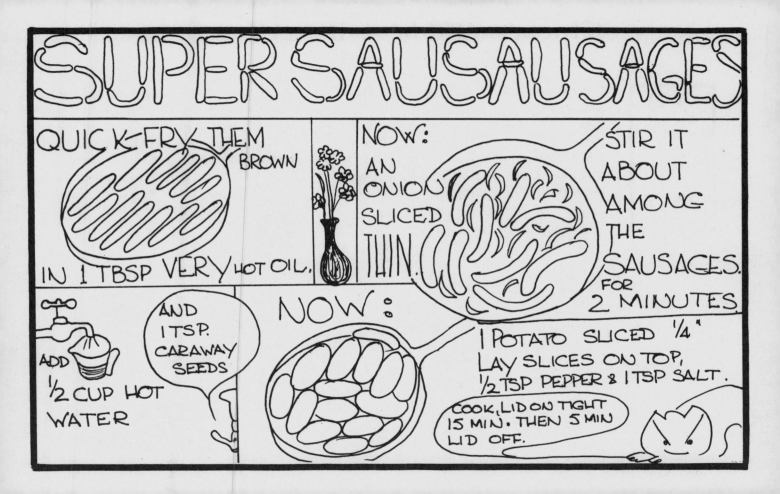

Chicken and Scotch

28

I really stole this recipe from the Four Seasons. We had just finished a twelve-hour stint in the studio, the lights had fried our brains, and what we needed was a rest. So we rented a suite with a big bath and a television set, a view of the mountains and room service.

After a bath, the champagne and some strawberries, we decided that room service was decadent, and went down to the dining room. And there it was, Chicken Breasts with Scotch, raising eyebrows among all the certified gourmets. It is simple and wonderful. If you don't like Scotch it tastes equally good with bourbon.

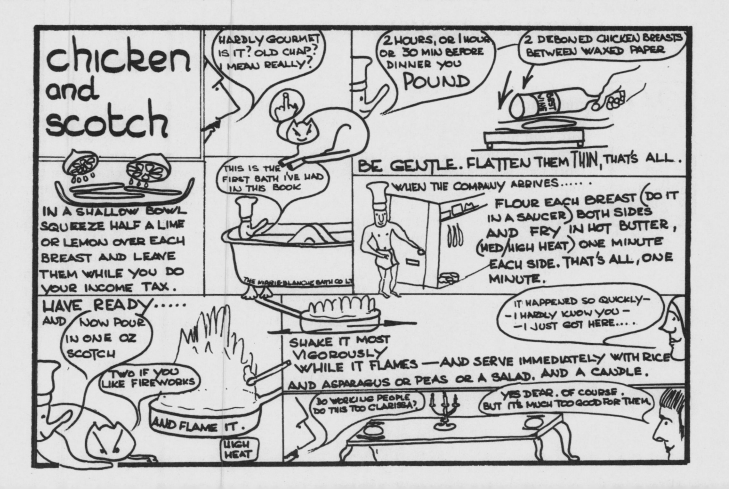

Garlic Chicken

Just don't tell 'em. Not unless you can trust 'em. You pick up a clove, put it close and squeeze the skin. The middle pops out into your mouth. It tastes as soft and gentle as lichee nuts, not at all like garlic. Once they get the feel of it they'll want more.

And garlic cooked in its skin is totally different from minced or chopped or pressed garlic. I frequently do it in stews – throw in two or three unpeeled cloves. They are easy to find and remove when you serve, especially when you have to lie a bit and tell them "No" when asked if there's garlic in it.

If you do think you smell a bit, the best thing is to start on your fingers, which you wash under a running cold tap. Hot water makes the oil go into your skin, cold rinses it away. On your breath a handful of parsley chewed well, or a belt of the freshest orange juice you can find. If there are two of you it shouldn't matter (because this is not the kind of dish you make for total strangers, and if there's a whole gang of you, then you can have a nice time discovering just how different it is from one person to another).

Don't be scared of garlic. There's nothing wrong with my social life.

Chicken and Tomatoes

This is the quickest and simplest dish I know. Colourful and bright, it never goes wrong, a Chinese dish which you can't get better even in a Chinese restaurant because the moment of truth comes from eating it the moment it's cooked.

Just get everybody ready, let them wait for you to get out of the bath, make your entrance, be calm, change the record, water a couple of plants, hum a bit, and if you have the kind of mate who asks, "What the hell do you think you're doing?" just say you're in an insouciant mood.

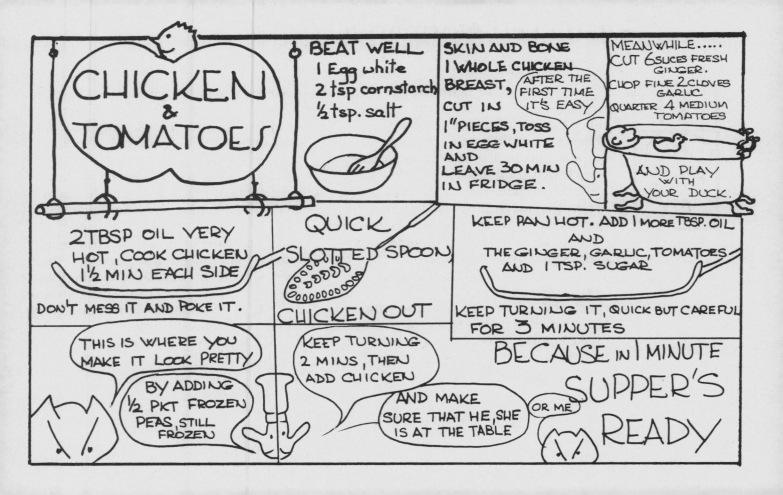

Chicken Normande

31

Calvados, the white lightning of Normandy, is a wonderful drink sometimes known in the U.S. as applejack. When I was riding a motorbike in one of our attempts to defend democracy the French would fill my waterbottle with Calvados (I could never figure out if this meant they were for me or agin me), frequent slugs of which made the pursuit of freedom and the life of a humble corporal considerably more bearable.

In the evening we would cook. We spent considerable time on a beach to which the U.S. Army had delivered vast quantities of canned chicken. Neighbouring beaches had equally vast quantities of canned peaches, and one beach was rumoured to have dried onions sufficient to supply the entire Allied Armies for six months. We ate canned chicken raw, cold, hot, lukewarm and with our fingers, and hated it. We drank the Calvados, which made us hate it a little less, but finally we discovered the value of combining the two.

Since that time I have refused (on deeply religious grounds) to have anything to do with canned chicken. But Calvados I'll drink any time. If you can't find Calvados, use rye, or bourbon; the apples and cream will make it almost as good. Particularly if you have a couple of belts while it's cooking.

Chicken and Rye

32

This happened one cold and windy night on Keats Island. We were well snugged up with the oil lamp going, a cribbage board and a bottle of Jack Daniels, rather hoping that the wind would get worse and nobody else would arrive, when about sixty feet of wall-to-wall fiberglass tied up across the float, complete, we later saw, with air conditioning, washer and dryer, television and a microwave oven.

Their generator had packed up. Could we heat them some water for instant coffee? We asked them for supper, and they arrived, most apologetically, with a bottle of Crown Royal, which, not to offend (and even more, not to deplete the Jack Daniels, which we figured to last a couple of days) we used to cook supper. They were delighted, and since then it has been a favourite, because most boats, like most well ordered houses, have a little rye around. It's even better with Jack Daniels. But so's just about everything.

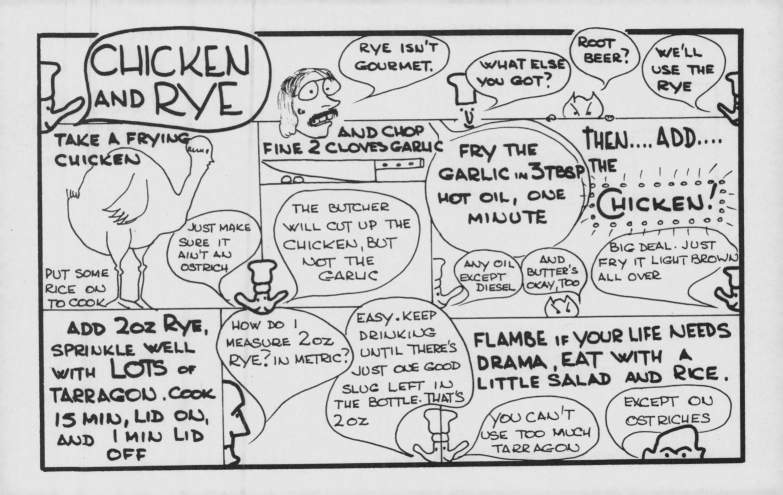

Pork Chops, mit Sort of Sauerkraut

33

Gourmet doesn't have to be wine. Sure, it's fine, those sauces of such elegance, and you can even make this with white wine if you want to. It won't taste the same – it will be different and it will be good, just as it will if you make it with chicken stock. But you don't have to have a Ph.D. in cork sniffing to be a good cook. The big test is the look on people's faces, and how much is left in the dish.

This is a fine, friendly supper for two, preferably two amiable, beer drinking, nicely tired people who have spent a good day together and don't want to wait too long before they spend a good night together.

We invented it one day in Degnen Bay after seven hours with the wind up our nose, victims of a schedule, sailing across the Strait of Georgia when we should have stayed tied to the wharf and in bed. She tidied the deck and lit the lamps; I cooked down below where it wasn't raining.

But it works equally well in a Montreal garret.

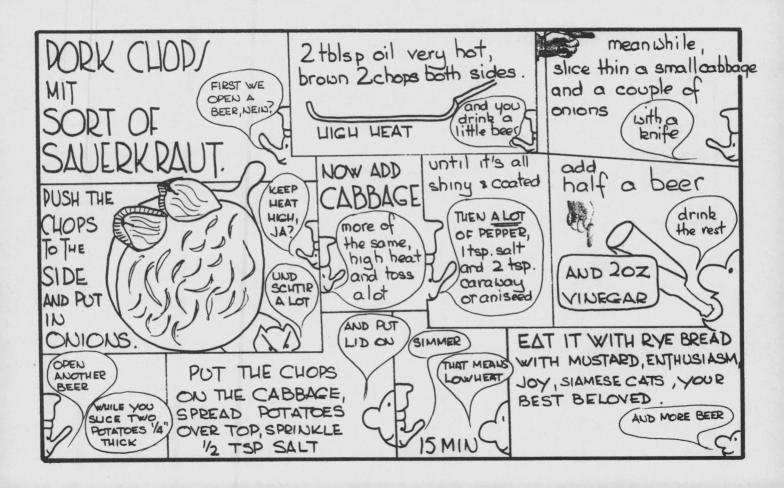

2 Beef Shanks, 2 Onions, 2 Hours

"Do we have to go out to a movie for this?"

"What do you mean?"

"Well, can we just stay home and watch TV?"

"Sure. But..."

"You don't want to watch TV?"

"Sure."

"You'd rather go to a movie?"

"No. TV's fine."

"So?"

"I haven't got a TV."

"Then I guess it's gotta be a movie."

"Does it have to have an airplane in it?"

"I don't think anyone will know. Besides, I'm going to use three teaspoons of that mustard left over from last week's hot dogs, instead of the dry mustard."

"You're a real daredevil, Fred."

"Wanna feel my muscle?"

"Let's go to the movie."

Oeufs Florentine

35

The French muck spinach about, they put cream in it and they grind it into baby food, they alter it and change it, beat it and butter it, until finally there is nothing of spinach about it, no green-leafed sunshine. It is nothing that grew in a garden and children looked at, nothing that a woman seven months pregnant might have picked for her man as a memory of the green grass they made the baby on.

Only the Japanese and the Italians understand spinach. Raw in a salad, with lemon juice, olive oil, a little green dill and, a finely chopped hard-boiled egg: that's okay, that's America's understanding of it, it's healthy and it's horny.

But most of the gourmet books insist that it be boiled into submission.

Oeufs Florentine is a gentle, soul-warming dish, very quick and easy, a perfect light lunch but an even better prescription for those dreadful days when nobody loves you and you feel like a Billie Holiday LP - "I Gotta Right to Sing the Blues...."

For a marvelous and unusual cold vegetable (which you can make the night before, or a couple of hours before) cook the spinach, drain it well in a colander, and shape it into long rolls about an inch in diameter. Sprinkle soy sauce on the rolls, then slice them carefully into pieces about an inch long (that way each is a mouthful), arrange prettily on a simple white plate, and let cool in the fridge for a while. Enjoy.

Huevos Rancheros

36

Brunch is disaster. We've all been sucked in by the *House and Garden* photographs of beautiful people, at ease in their caftans, leisure suits and ear-to-ear smiles, while host and hostess graciously dispense Tequila Sunrises.

Brunch in fact leads to divorce. Nobody wants to be settled for life with somebody offering rubber eggs, cardboard bacon, apathetic toast and tired coffee. Eggs Benedict, that staple of bourgeois brunches, usually ends in total disaster, harsh words in the kitchen, the guests leaving early and saying much too brightly, "How marvelous, darling, how terribly clever of you." And even before the car door is closed one of them says, "Let's not send *them* a Christmas card."

This is a no-nonsense brunch, eminently suitable for a very limited kitchen. You can make the sauce the night before and with a good big pan you can cook eight eggs at a time.

And what goes best with Huevos Rancheros is beer. Mexican beer is best, and that's how I first ate it, dreadfully hung over one morning in Santo Tomás, a long cold beer before, one with and two or three afterwards, while we watched, on the other side of the road, a man quietly and competently shave a twenty-foot pole into long slivers, which he then made into a basket and sold for a dollar, after which he got on his horse and rode off.

If you have a spare green pepper, slice it thin and put it in the sauce. You can then call it Piperade, and pretend you are in the South of France. If you have any sauce left, thin it out a bit next day, throw in a soup cube and you have a marvellous quick soup.

Vegetables Vegetables Vegetables

Like the backs of seventeen-year-old knees. Plump and fair and fresh. You have to enjoy vegetables, despite the attempts of the supermarkets to plasticize the experience. All the squeezing (ever watched people putting the half nelson on an avocado?) doesn't really tell you anything; the look should be enough, unless it's a melon you're after, when you have to pick it up and smell it, stick it right under your nose and smell the blunt end, sniff out the perfume – all that genetic inheritance of some distant Persian garden filled with dark-eyed ladies, flying carpets, big black eunuchs with scimitars and an aged gardener sitting quietly in the corner smoking his *bhang*.

Remember too the Chinese way and don't overcook them. Frozen vegetables are half-digested when you open the packet, so particularly don't overcook them.

I never defrost frozen peas – just dump them straight into the dish – unless I put an ounce of butter in a small saucepan, line it with lettuce leaves, dump in the peas, sprinkle with salt and pepper and a good half teaspoon of dried mint (or some fresh mint leaves), put on the lid and cook at medium heat, shaking frequently, for six or seven minutes.

And rutabagas, those big old yellow old turnips that nobody buys (they keep them in the supermarkets just to confuse the cost of living index) are badly neglected. Eat them raw in thin strips with soy sauce, or mash them with an equal quantity of mashed potatoes, lots of butter and maybe a beaten egg, lots of pepper and some salt.

Enjoy, enjoy, enjoy.

VEGETABLE VEGETABLES VEGETABLES VEGETABLES VEGETABLES VEGETABLES

CARROTS:
CUT LENGTHWISE INTO 1/4" STRIPS. SPRINKLE SUGAR. COOK IN 1TBSP BUTTER, 1/2 CUP WATER 1/2 TSP SALT. TURN OFTEN WHEN WATER EVAPORATED. MED HEAT. ABOUT 6 MINUTES

PARSNIPS THIS WAY TOO

FANTASTIC

BROCCOLI
CUT INTO PIECES THIS BIG. 1/4" WATER IN PAN, BOIL, BROCCOLI IN, SPRINKLE SALT, COOK 3 MIN. LID ON

DRAIN & TOSS IN BASIC VINAIGRETTE (PAGE 12) WITH OREGANO. EAT & ENJOY. HOT.

GET A SHARP KNIFE. USE STALKS TOO

ZUCCHINI:
1/2" SLICES. FRY HIGH HEAT 2 MIN EACH SIDE, WITH CHOP'D GARLIC. THEN SPRINKLE SALT, JUICE 1/2 LEMON, LID ON TIGHT, LOW HEAT, 10 MIN.

< 1/2" > < 1/2" > < 1/2" >

1/2" SLICES RIGHT?

RUTABAGAS
TRY THIS: PEEL, CUT IN 1 1/2" CHUNKS. BOIL (A LITTLE SALT), 15 MIN. DRAIN WELL, MASH WITH LOTS OF BUTTER, LOTS OF PEPPER AND AN EGG YOLK. (MORE SALT)

NOBODY EATS RUTABAGAS

EVEN I LOVE THIS ONE

Tsalad de Tsupermarket de Tsawwassen

You have to toss it, and you don't put the dressing on until a minute before you serve it, and before that you have to have the bread ready and the appetites polished and everybody watching, because it looks nice if you've built it carefully, and as you shove your spoons down the bottom of the bowl and turn up the hidden treasures they are immediately appreciative, just as they are in fancy restaurants when the waiter comes and makes da bigga da fuss with the Caesar Salad.

This is a good summer-day supper, very wholesome with a glass of milk if you want to stay holy. You can equally well be sitting on a fire escape or a 47th-storey lakeside patio. A salad like this and a decent hamburger (page 16) make a princely meal. (In fact, if any of the princes who visit us have to eat the same rubber chicken as I get served at official functions, then it is a much more than princely meal.)

Tsawwassen? Some of *them* pronounce it Sawwassen, and tsome of them insist on T-sawassen. It's in the tsouthwest corner of British Columbia, and is famous for being a five-minute ride from Point Roberts, Washington State's Tijuana.

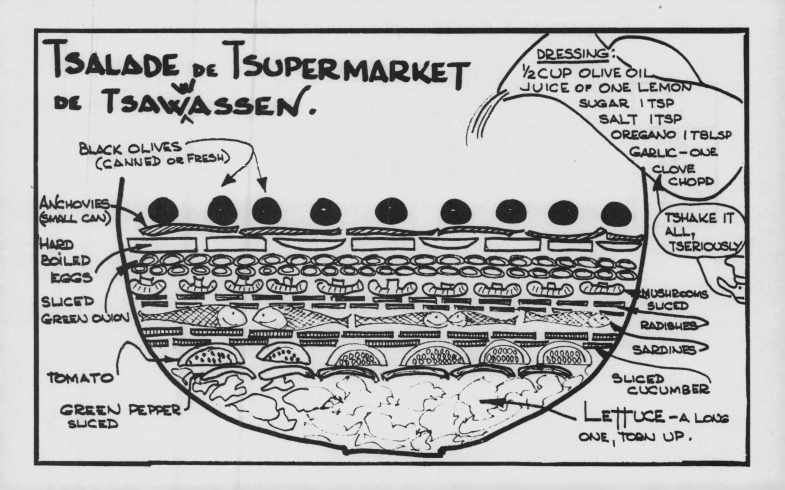

Candid Bananas

Candid. Up front. Open. Honest. This is a dessert ridiculously simple, disgustingly rich, gloriously calorific and, because of the ready availability of bananas, habit forming. Just be a little careful, don't have the heat too high, take them out of the pan with the same care you would offer   a day-old baby (anybody who has ever car- ried a baby about on a spoon will know exactly what I mean) and serve them on warm plates. Don't cook too many at a time; three bananas is enough for the average pan, and besides, it does your guests good to wait for seconds. And thirds.

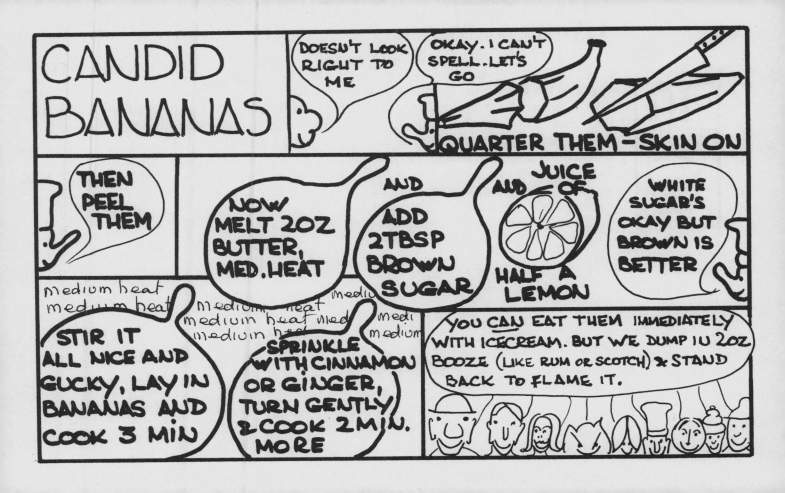

Oyster Stew

40

You can eat them with crushed caviar on top; you can also order them Oysters Provençale, Oysters Maréchale, Oysters Tetrazzini, Oysters Poulette, Oysters Rockefeller and Oysters Kirkpatrick. There is no end of the oyster recipes of the world. All the major coastal cuisines favour them and all seem to share the same belief that they are aphrodisiac.

Brillat-Savarin figured that everything was aphrodisiac. Everything edible, that is. He called it the *sens génésique*, or the sense of the learned taste buds.

Be nice to this one. Rarely can you be kind to yourself in only five minutes.

Piccata di Vitello

James, will you marry me?

I had never been proposed to by a man before, it was the end of my first show with Peter Gzowski and in fourteen minutes (because rice takes that long to cook) we had made a whole dinner, all of it on a two-burner pump-up stove. We had soup, and this Piccata di Vitello, and asparagus, and the rice bright yellow and delightful, and dessert, and coffee. And we got hundreds of letters.

We had never cooked together before, there was no rehearsal, no back-up kitchen, no special facilities – just a Coleman camp stove, a fry pan, a coffee pot (in which we cooked the coffee and the asparagus) and a little saucepan for the soup.

The recipe in the drawing uses chicken breasts because they are cheaper than veal. I use veal because that is the classic basis of this dish, and there is a special marriage between veal, butter and lemon, something super-rich. It is the sort of dish that only the very best of restaurants would dare serve because it is so simple, like most of the great secrets of the world.

If you want to tart it up a little, throw in a handful of smallish mushrooms (the white ones, cut in half) when the white wine goes in. And if you want to make the rice a colour spectacular, throw a teaspoon of turmeric (very cheap, not like saffron) into the water and stir in a handful of very finely cut green onions just before you serve it.

The Ultimate Simplicity

42

Every Wednesday night in the logging camp we got sausage and cabbage. The cook said it was a Ukrainian dish. He was Chinese. The other nights we got chicken and steak and pork chops, but Wednesday night was the one we looked forward to.

A great supper for poker night, the day before payday, Grey Cup parties. And kids like it too.

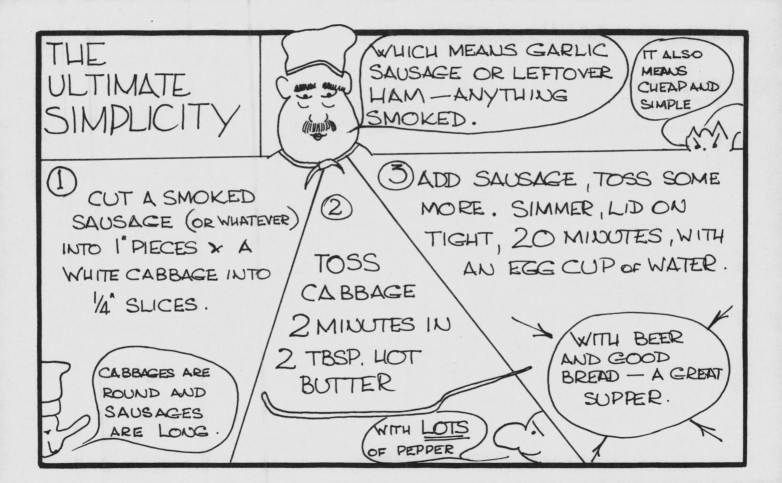

Lamb Shanks

43

Hot lamb roast on Sundays, cold on Mondays, minced on Tuesdays, and curried on Wednesdays – I was raised on lamb.

It seems, in retrospect, to have been nothing on Thursdays, fish of course on Friday, scrambled eggs on Saturday, and then it was Sunday all over again, and more lamb.

There was so much of it. Like the Christmas turkey, it went on forever. Lamb shanks are a way out. They are cheap, easy to figure out mathematically (one lamb shank, one person; two lamb shanks, two persons – you don't need a calculator) and they are infinitely variable. Lamb takes kindly to thyme, sage, oregano, parsley, curry powder, tomatoes, almost anything if you remember that if it doesn't taste exactly right what you have forgotten is the lemon.

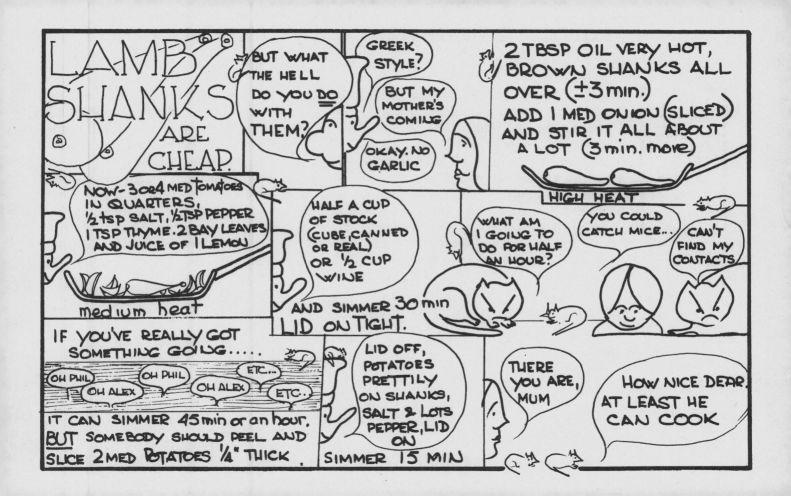

Tortilla Española

Hot, cold or lukewarm, the Spanish tortilla (which has nothing at all to do with the Mexican tortilla) is always good. Spanish women are known for their tortillas, in much the same way as, a few years ago, country women were known for their cakes. The simplest of all, with potatoes, is a great favourite in tapas bars, served cold in wedges with rich, rough red wines. Once you have mastered the art (much of which lies in flipping the tortilla over the plate) then you can experiment on your own, because basically this is a country dish, not a haute cuisine gourmet number, and it makes use of whatever is around. By the time you've tried a little broccoli in it, or maybe some spinach, it probably will have evolved into an Italian frittata, and with a little chopped bacon it gets to be a Denver sandwich. But it's cheap, and it's quick, and it keeps – the ideal quick dish with which to impress visitors and still have a bit left over for the next day.

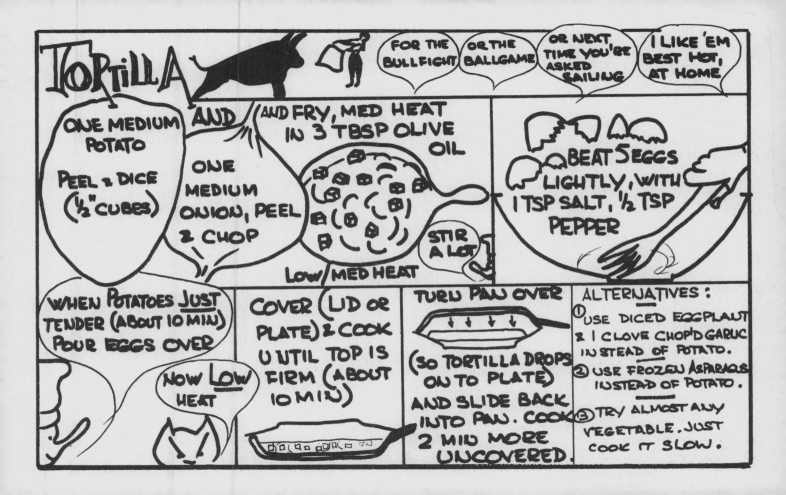

Index